End of Life Stories

TIPS AND TOOLS FOR THE SOULS JOURNEY HOME

Cindy Bertrand Larson

Artwork by Louis Larson

◆ FriesenPress

Suite 300 - 990 Fort St
Victoria, BC, V8V 3K2
Canada

www.friesenpress.com

Thank you Lou Larson for the gift of your artwork.

Thank you to the clients, patients, friends and family who are my teachers as I Journey Home. This book would not be possible without you.

ISBN
978-1-77097-244-5 (Hardcover)
978-1-77097-245-2 (Paperback)
978-1-77097-246-9 (eBook)

1. FAMILY & RELATIONSHIPS, ELDERCARE

Distributed to the trade by The Ingram Book Company

For my Grandma Olga.

Thank you for saving my life more than once.
You are a very good guardian angel.

See you at the bus stop.

Contents

Tips and Tools For The Soul's Journey Home

Introduction

They began as soft proddings waking me in the night. "Tell them about the man who, at ninety, picked up a paintbrush and created stunning paintings, greeting cards, and inspiration for other seniors," one says. "Tell them the story about the lady on the second floor of the facility, the one who takes a pill for the depression draping her life, a woman lonely and aching with certainty she will never again smell the prairie air from her farmhouse veranda," goes another.

Ah, yes, those soft, friendly whispers that soon turned into downright bossy demands. "Write the book already," they said. "People need to know they have choices, tools, and support. Let people know they are not alone when they fear pain while dying and that becoming a burden tops the list of what people don't want at the end of their life."

Caring for people as they journey home has taught me to trust, trust, trust the process called life. I am now able to walk at the pace of certainty, to listen with my heart, and to communicate from my soul. I am blessed to have witnessed some very good deaths.

If we know death is coming, we have time to prepare. With the intention of cleaning the slate before we go, we forgive past grievances, correct miscommunications, clear up unresolved issues, and make the *space within* ready for what's to come next.

My ears have heard the anguished cry of a person arriving at the bedside of a deceased person too late, wishing they had said sorry for things from long ago. I have witnessed difficult passing's, where family members squabbling over childhood leftovers have been unable to rise above judgement, expectations, and the need to be right. I have seen the thick strain of complicated grief shatter family unity, scattering people to the wind like brittle leaves.

We can choose to be uplifted by death, to allow it to be our teacher, to make us better, more compassionate, and willing to live awake. Walking that way takes courage; the stones unturned are reminders that we don't know the way. We can also choose to fear death, to try and outwit it or outrun it; to pretend it doesn't belong to us.

Preparing to die can look like a lot of different things. It might look like gathering your children in your home for a Chinese food dinner to tell them how much you love them. It might look like calling a sibling to open doors of communication and to try, one more time, from a different perspective. It may involve taking a fearless inventory, forgiving yourself and others, and letting life be what it is without judgement or expectation.

A very important *key to living* came to me by way of a dying person I never met. At a hospice seminar, a woman shared a story about her husband, who was in the last days of his life. Coming into his room, she found him sitting at the side of the bed, staring at the floor, shaking his head, and saying something about mankind having it all wrong. "What do we have all wrong?" she asked him, shocked to find him conscious and speaking. "*It's about the intention of the love we put into every moment of living,*" he told her. These powerful words rolled off her tongue toward me and landed in my heart with a thud. *Love with intentionality.*

The purpose in writing this book is to encourage you to clean up, clear out, heal, and resolve any outstanding issues you have. You can only do this today in the present. To wait until death hovers, weighing you down with the heaviness of unexpressed forgiveness is a mistake.

As you read the tips and tools section, pay attention if you become irritated by the invitation to think differently and notice when you go into resistance. As we embrace another way of seeing things, the beliefs we hold too tightly may feel under siege. The tips and tools are helpful suggestions and ideas to help you expand into a more conscious self. Give yourself time to ponder the questions, paying special attention to when you feel the need to be right. Enjoy the process. Give it respect, time, and mindfulness.

During the most difficult times in life, we may need support because we do not know the way. Be brave and reach out to a trusted professional counsellor, therapist, friend, or family member.

Don't be afraid, either, to cultivate a relationship with God, whatever that is for you. We all belong to this great mystery called life, and from its beginning to end, we are watched over, guided toward our potential, and loved by something unseen. Honoring that relationship will enhance the quality of your life and make the end of life an adventure.

Let this book be a light by which you can better see your way.

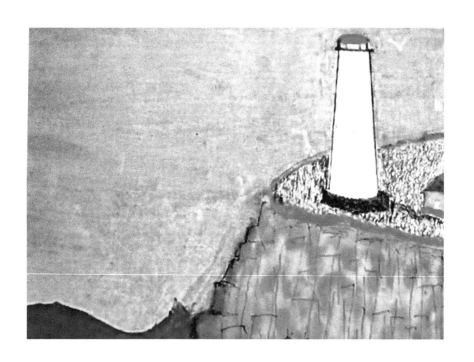

Who are you then?

When your body forces you to surrender your favorite food, drink, habit, job, or person, your golf game, bridge game, painting sessions, piano playing, and sex, who will you become? When you give up what you love the most after having given everything you can, who are you then? When you sit alone in a room and no one knows you or remembers what a great teacher, boss, father, husband, or mother you have been, who are you then? When you are at the mercy of the system, left to be cared for by people who are strangers what does your soul resonate; what prayer does your heart ache for? After giving everything to life, only to have it taken from you, as you sit in the silence of an unfamiliar room with only your clouded memories, who are you then?

What dies before the body dies?
What is the gift in the suffering?
Who is left behind? What did they give? What did they get?
How did the gift of suffering make them better people?

Chapter One

My First Client, May: *The way we do small things is the way we do big things*

When I began my career as a caregiver, my first job was to prepare dinner and spend the night with a ninety-year-old Dutch woman who felt safer with someone there as she slept. Decades earlier, her husband had built a beautiful cedar home looking over rolling hills of fertile valley. He had been a prisoner of war, and they had come to this country because the dry air was good for his ailing health. He died on the couch in their home and, for that reason, as I learned over time, May wanted to die in their home, too. My job at the time, I thought, was to be of good food service and safety for her.

Like so many unexpected, perfectly suitable circumstances in our lives, this experience was about to change me in ways I didn't know I needed.

After many months of caring for May, I came in one winter evening to find her crouched under the cupboards, pulling out various containers, pans, and casserole dishes. "This is not mine", she would say handing me some antique pot. "Does this belong to you?"

"Nope, not mine" I would say, taking it from her and placing it to the side with the collection of other items, none of them, she insisted, hers, all mysteries for the way they'd made their way into her cupboards.

May was tiny, strong, and disciplined. She had forged through the Second World War eating tulip bulbs and was not the least bit reserved about counting the cutlery in front of me as I prepared to leave for the day. On preparing her dinner one evening, I placed baby carrots side by side on her plate and, although I had intended for them to be received as angels, her response was, "Oh, look. Soldiers." The war, what it took from her family, and the pain it caused her personally was part of our daily conversation. I was curious about her experiences and she was happy to share, becoming more animated, passionately flailing her arms in between sips of a very strong port, telling stories as if for the first time.

May read *The New York Times* once a week and watched the news daily to keep current. Not fond of gooey hellos or hugging, she held her own ground while looking you up and down to make sure you were professionally groomed.

May's children wanted her to come live with them in Europe, but her choice was to be independent and stay in Canada, to live and die in the house her husband had built for them. In response to the loving invitation from her children, she quipped, "Why would I go put myself into a position where my children can tell me where to live, what to eat, and what time to go to bed? I didn't live this long to give up myself at the end."

It was about eight o'clock on a drizzly spring evening and we were sitting on the couch after a nice dinner when, suddenly, with a jolt and a spasm, May fell back onto the couch, turned white, and retreated into herself. The ambulance arrived and took her to the hospital. She was conscious, but very frail.

"What do you want us to do if she needs to be revived?" The doctor asked, presuming I was May's daughter.

"I don't know," I told them. "I'm her caregiver and all her family is abroad."

May turned to me and expressed an inkling of vulnerability. "What should I do? I don't want to live and spend the rest of my life in a bed, dying." We called the children, each one knowing this may be the last time they ever talk with their mother. During the conversation with her two daughters, May was listless and weak. When we finally reached her son by phone, May bolted straight up in her bed and began to shout at him. She was really giving him the what-for. I don't know what she said because she was speaking in Dutch, but whatever it was, it got her up and paying attention. There was a lot more respect going around that emergency room for May after she declared herself *the matriarch*.

The next day, May was transferred from the emergency room to a shared room on the second floor. She was only there a short time when a nurse came in to fit her for an oxygen mask. Without any resistance or fanfare, May fraily declined, turned over on her side, and died.

What is so interesting is that May's heart attack on the couch was in the exact same place where her husband had passed away a decade earlier.

At the funeral, May's children spoke of her seemingly hands-off approach to parenting. Theirs was not a household where mother was shouting "I love you!" as they headed out the door to school.

Still, each child spoke of how much love she had for them. They could feel it in the effort she made to call them to task, to show up, and to be their best. She was that tough-love kind of a lady and you never really knew if she liked you; it didn't seem to matter as much as receiving her respect, which could only be achieved by ruthless adherence to her structure and requests.

She was a taskmaster for sure, expecting things to be folded perfectly, polished immaculately, and done on time. She didn't teach by expecting you to do the tasks; her teaching was one of an invitation. If you wanted to participate in this game of "doing things a certain way," you had to really want to, and be willing to learn how to do things in a way that was acceptable to her. Otherwise, you were invited to *not* participate.

The truth is, I was afraid of May at first. I had never met someone so unapologetically direct. She was not concerned about people's feelings. She was aiming much higher than trying not to offend. May was ruthless in a loving way, and I learned that her words were meant to make better—not tear down. In those few years with May, I learned how to communicate what I need clearly, without a lot of drama. She wore the "circling in flight, never landing on an opinion so I will be liked by everyone" quality right out of me.

Helping me become a better person is not something May intentionally set out to do. It was a slow, grinding away of the unworkable that saw me finally succumb to the right way. Her strength rubbed off on others, too. And even if it looked a bit scratchy at the onset of one's change, if you hung in there, something wonderful would come of you under her watchful eye. Life sometimes presents itself inside out and upside down. I thought I was going to take care of a frail little old lady. It turned out I was tutored in how to be a lady, unafraid to be herself and strong enough to carry others to the starting line of a better self, as well.

It's been over a decade since I said goodbye to May, but I still hear her voice telling me to refold that towel right. She impacted my life not by what she said, but by *how* she did what she did, and who she was. It isn't just the towels that I fold correctly; it's the way I dress myself, taking care to present myself in a way that invites respect. May has impacted the way I drive, eat, cook, and work with others. I say less, and listen more.

The biggest life-changing lesson I learned from May? That the way we do the small things is the way we do everything!

ꝳ Questions to Consider

Who in your life has challenged you to a higher standard and encouraged you to become your best?

How did you feel about them at that time? How do you feel about them now? What is the posture you are taking regarding that person? Are you:

- In resistance?
- Fearful?
- Accommodating?

- Respectful?
- Defiant?
- Grateful?

Find a quiet place where you can close your eyes and breathe into what you are experiencing. Take notice of where in your body you are feeling sensations. Give them permission to be there. Give the process respect and listen to your inner dialogue. Don't argue, justify, or judge the experience. It's about you learning to feel what you feel and be OK with your truth. As you exhale, thank the people, places, and situations that have somehow challenged you to become the best possible version of yourself.

Chapter Two

Luigi's Long Life: You're never too old

Luigi fathered seven children. He was born with an entrepreneurial nature that allowed him to provide for his family and enabled him to travel and work all over the world. Once, I served him and his wife chili in a restaurant and if you'd told me then that, one day, I'd be their daughter-in-law, I'd have called you crazy. Luigi was in his eighties when I met him. With grown children with their own families, he and his lovely wife lived in an upscale seniors' retirement center. For years, he organized bingo games for his community. He put in a golf putting green, as well, and was the go-to guy for others where he lived. Then his wife passed away and there was a void in his life. His family and friends talked about how we might help him enjoy his remaining time.

Luigi would often doodle on scraps of paper. We took little notice until, one day, we had a conversation about art. I painted and drew myself and derived great pleasure from it. On our next visit to Luigi, we brought paints, canvasses, brushes, pencils, and conversations about how art is a wonderful way to pass the time.

Now, instead of Luigi complaining about not being able to get around as he used to and needing the assistance of a walker, he was content to sit at his table and paint. At the beginning, we complimented his efforts and were genuinely impressed with his pieces, as a talented artist emerged from within his being. He was ninety when he touched his first art tools and, by the time he finished his last piece, he had created over twenty beautiful works of art. They were all different: portraits, landscapes, flowers, and scenes from his travels.

We thought we were helping this elderly man pass his time, but little did we know what was about to happen. Pretty soon, Luigi was receiving attention for his creations. People began to stop by, interested in what his latest canvas would bear. Then the seniors' center where he lived came to life with the buzz that Luigi was going to have an art showing. The newspaper did a front-page story with a big photo of him and a caption that read "You're Never Too Old." The television station came to interview this totally inspiring individual who was now encouraging other seniors to live more fully. Luigi had a following of people who wanted to know what would be on his pallet next. The acknowledgement he received fueled his life with meaning and purpose.

At his show, the room exuded festivity. Original framed pieces hung on the walls, and those members of the public who were interested in the arts milled about the room with paper and pencil in hand. They each marked their three favorites, and provided an explanation on why they had been moved by them. Luigi's art reminded people of places long ago when they had danced, fished, walked in nature, or sat in awe. In the center of the room, Luigi looked like a king. The most popular piece he painted was the winter cabin on the lake scene, included in this book.

Luigi was a gift giver. He was always handing you something he had purchased or found or created to make the day a little brighter. We—his family and friends—were constantly interested in his next offering. But we began to see the meat melt from his bones. His dentures now seemed loose, the belt that held up his pants needed more tightening. We were forever suggesting he eat more, and brought root beer ice cream floats, snacks, and energy shakes to see it through.

The walk to the dining room that used to be a graceful skip with his wife was now met with trepidation. "I only have so many more steps," he'd concede, his blue eyes softly shining. He knew we were hurting. We knew he was hurting, too. The cancer that had been for so long kept at bay was now ready to challenge us all. And then he announced, "This is my last piece." He painted the Pyrenees mountains, the majesty and magic having stayed with him from decades earlier when he'd been there building a road. Luigi built roads and bridges all over the world and now he'd built a different kind of bridge for others to walk across. It was a bridge of belief. Just because someone is elderly doesn't mean they have nothing to offer. He put love into the last chapter of his life, not self-pity.

"So, do your feet and legs hurt?" asked his doctor. We knew the answer as we had asked it many times ourselves. Luigi was a polio victim and plane crash survivor, an episode that had left him with a crooked, broken back. He never complained about pain and would often react to the question of his discomfort with a look of surprise. "Who, me, in pain?" he'd respond. "No. Not at all." On this day, the answer was different. "It only hurts when I walk," he said.

Thus, the scramble to manage Luigi's pain began. Family members now wheeled him to the dining room, where he ate nothing or only bird-sized samplings of food. Then the trips to the dining room stopped, and meal trays were brought into his room. The wheel of life was spinning more slowly now, an inevitability that was met with a predictable array of his family's emotions. First, there was denial. "The cancer can be treated. Let's find him different medicine." That was followed by anger at the situation itself, then blame. We blamed the doctors, the system, the caregivers, and life itself for the inevitable. After that, the bargaining began. "If he can just do one more painting, just make it to Christmas, we promise to be satisfied." But life and death do not bargain. They have their own agenda and it is we who must adjust. Depression was the undercurrent as we dealt with our own helplessness and questioned how we could have done more, been more, given more. Then came *our* acceptance that Luigi would paint no more.

Luigi's hospice room was full of flowers: beautiful red roses, sunflowers, daisies, and freesias. The TV played his favorite sports channel. His sons had placed some of his art on the walls along with a family portrait from decades earlier. One time, he looked out at the garden and announced that his wife was standing there, looking in, waiting patiently. Instead of letting the pain of separation destroy the last years of his life because he loved her so, Luigi painted his grief away. How it looked to the rest of the world was splendid, powerful, majestic, tender, and beautiful.

Friends who were too old or ill to travel called or Skyped in to see him one last time. Luigi never did get the concept that an iPad was not a phone. He would grab the machine and put it to his ear to talk and listen, sending the rest of us into correction mode. "Oh, no, Luigi. When you put your face right up close like that, they can only see your ear." It was confusing for him because the computer age was not a place in which he was comfortable, although he did get to see his website, which hosted his greeting cards and TV interview. His eldest son, in hospital himself miles away, called in to have a final conversation. Others drove hundreds of miles to tell him what a difference he had made in their lives.

A kind woman minister arrived mid-day and asked Luigi if he was ready to go to the next place. With his family surrounding him with baited breath, he gently spoke, "yes." The nurses made Luigi comfortable. His family hovered and recanted stories of days gone by.

Luigi could have gone out to pasture meekly, surrendering to his grief, falling into helplessness as he struggled to be mobile, turning into the deep of himself, never to be retrieved. Instead, Luigi gave what he had left of his life force to the world as an example.

The night Luigi passed, his son recalls a remarkable vision in the sky. Well after midnight, far from the glaring lights of the city, two parallel columns of what looked like clouds spiraled their way up to the stars. It was the great mystery silently receiving Luigi and his wife, who had been patiently waiting for him to finish playing with his paints.

𝆺 Questions to Consider

Is there something you have wanted to do your whole life but believe yourself too old or fear being judged by yourself or others if you tried? Will you consider replacing that belief system with something more empowering? We limit ourselves when we make decisions based on other people's opinions. Perhaps it's time to reach out, to expand our belief systems, and embrace the potential of the undiscovered self. What is the first step for you?

Chapter Three

Goodbye, Grace: Suspending judgement and asking the right questions

"What do you want? Oh, it's *you!*" she snarled, and went back to her knitting. The appearance of a half a watermelon and a spoon turned this ninety-three-year-old into a little kid. "Watermelon!"

Grace enthusiastically dug into the melon while I checked her kitchen to see what kind of shape it was in. It's common for seniors to sometimes forget to close the freezer door, or leave the stove on with or without something cooking. My job was to support this lovely, little, often irritable, lady, so she could stay in her home.

Grace was angry that she needed help, and frustrated that she was constantly being interrupted by neighbors and I looking in on her to make sure she was OK. She enjoyed her own company and seemed content to knit and watch old movies while eating a can of salmon for dinner. Who knew what secrets she would not tell that were dormant in her memory bank. Whatever had happened in her life had left some scars that still caused her pain. She did not speak of her Second World War experiences or how she had ended up alone in a small town.

When you gave Grace the time and she was sure you weren't going to run off mid-story, she would look you straight in the eyes and say something profound. "You know what?" With just a twinkle of approval, she would launch into fascination. "Do you believe in UFOs?" she asked me one day.

Tingling from head to toe, I told her, "Yes, I do!" Now that the water was safe and she had an audience, her eyes bulged out. "Well, I saw one once. I was living up the valley a few hours and it was dusk. I had a big bag of garbage in my hand and was taking it to the dumpster. As I got to the top of the hill, this big spaceship moved slowly in front of me. I stood there for a long time. Then it silently moved away. When I got home, I told my husband and he said that I was full of it. So, I took out a piece of paper and drew it for him."

"Can you draw it for me?" I asked, as I scrambled for a blank piece of paper. What she drew was astounding: a perfect triangle shape with lights all around the perimeter, able to fly up and down, back and forth, like a dragonfly or a hummingbird. She said it was perfectly silent. I believed her, because she was telling the truth. Grace did not lie.

Grace often took to her bed for weeks, and we presumed she would pass in her home. On a recent trip to the hospital, she was adamant. "I told you, doctor, I'm getting out of here right now!" Sure enough, she went home with a report that nothing could be found to keep her there. "Oh, geez, I'm old," she would scowl, searing your soul with her blue eyes.

After a stint in the hospital, the integration process could be a bit of a challenge, especially in the morning. The first thing Grace did upon such a day was dismiss me. She snapped that she didn't want breakfast or anything else and to just get out would be perfect. One of the things I learned along the way is that "*the quality of my life depends on the questions I ask,*" so I breathed deeply and made my request silently: "How can I reach Grace, get her care done, and leave her happy?" Within a split second, my emotional literacy kicked in and I bellowed like a drill sergeant, "Look, Grace. I know you went through a lot in the war and I know you don't like being old. I know you don't like going to the hospital and I know you don't like my coming over here to help you. I get it, Grace. But it's not my fault! I care about you very much, Grace, so for goodness' sake, let me help you with your medicines and eye drops and getting you dressed, then I will get the heck out!" Something about the directness of that leveled the playing field. She sat up and we completed the morning tasks. When I left, she grumbled a "thank you" with a dash of eye contact, and our relationship was forever changed for the better.

Toward the end of her time, Grace softened. "Do you think I should go to the hospital?" she would ask me. "Do you think you need to go?" I would gently question back. "Well, maybe," she'd respond, looking down at her knitting needles. This time we did call, and the dedicated, smiling faces of the paramedics, all dressed in blue, arrived in short order. "Good day, Grace. How can we help you today?" She was a frequent guest in their ambulance. I did not know that when they drove away with her that time, she would never return home.

After a few weeks in the hospital, Grace went to a seniors' facility about 200 miles south. She did not particularly like the town and knew no one there. I wanted to drive up and say hello to her one day, but that would have made her cringe. Grace used anger as a protective mechanism. If you brought flowers during a hospital visit, she would shout at you, "What did you bring me them for? I don't want 'em." If you had a watermelon or fish-and-chip offering, you were a friend until the next time. And if you showed any sign of weakness, you were toast. One of the most admirable things about Grace was her inner strength. She attributed her physical strength to the UFO experience. "Those guys did something to me. I should be dead by now. I've had five heart attacks!"

I don't know all the details of Grace's history—they are gone with her ashes—but I am in awe of who Grace became in her life. She was a brave soldier, an independent woman, a mother, elder, and citizen who belonged to us all. She was not the warmest person, yet her love shone through and she was deeply inspiring for those of us who took her seriously. Her sharp sense of humor and quick wit with a glint of sparkly sarcasm will always bring a smile to my face as I remember her *not* looking up when you entered the room. This was her territory and you were lucky to be in it. Have a seat.

✗ Questions to Consider

If the quality of our life can be enhanced by the questions we ask, what questions are appropriate for you to ask yourself right now? Suggestions are in the Tips and Tools section.

JOSHUA 1: 9

HAVE I NOT
COMMANDED YO
BE STRONG &
COURAGEOUS.
DO NOT BE
TERRIFIED, do
NOT BE discourag
FOR THE LORD YOU
God WILL BE WIT
YOU WHEREVER
YOU GO.

Chapter Four

Adam: *Following my father home*

As the seven of us stood around my father on his death bed, there was an unmistakable sense of his spirit hovering and lifting off. We could feel it, like a current of energy moving, dancing almost, as it ascended. For more than an hour, we surrounded him like a wagon train, looking at each other with astonishment, shaking our heads with curiosity. Dad's spirit had texture, like sticky wind, and it moved up like a spiral, ever so slowly. It seemed to have a knowledge about where it was going.

I had left home four decades earlier, never to return except for summer-vacation visits. Now witnessing my father leaving his body, I remembered how, ten years earlier when my life had fallen apart, I had driven across the country depressed and broken. Upon arriving at Dad's home, I felt the struggle cease and my suffering surrender itself into acceptable reconciliation and peace. I hoped Dad would experience that same comfort and relief when he arrived at his spirit home.

My father had changed so much in the time I was away living my life and raising my own family, thousands of miles away. His days were filled with delivering food hampers to those in need and taking disabled children for horseback-riding adventures. Dads mornings were spent reading scriptures and asking what he could bring to the day.

During those ten years, I would watch my father a few pews ahead of me in church. He would sit leaning forward, elbows on his knees, hands clutched, head down. He was asking for forgiveness for all he had done and not done. He was showing me what it looked like to surrender my mistakes, to own them and heal my life.

Only three months earlier, my sister and I, sitting in the waiting room of the doctor's office, had breathed a sigh of relief. Dad walked out with a smile on his face. "Let's go to the house and order some Chinese food," he said. Once home, he removed a little piece of paper from his pocket and put it on the counter. I could tell by the way he patted it down that it meant something to him. With Dad's permission, I photographed what he wrote and the words are now on my cell phone and on the backs of pictures and cards that I send out to people.

Joshua 1:9: Have I not commanded you be strong and courageous. Do not be terrified, do not be discouraged, for the Lord your God is with you wherever you are.

Over dinner that night, Dad informed the family that he had a form of leukemia and that blood transfusions were going to help keep him alive. We four kids and spouses were all happy to support this new experience. Outings to the hospital could be an adventure. We tried to put a happy face on the experience until after his fourth transfusion. The transfusions were keeping Dad alive, but only for short periods of time. They made him feel sickly after—hung over, he said—and he was so tired he could barely walk. Soon after Dad stopped the transfusions, confusion set in. He got his days and nights mixed up and was prone to falling. We called the hospice nurse.

As we waited for the nurse to arrive, I sat in between two worlds. My father was in the living room on a couch, covered in blankets, fidgeting and moaning, his spirit struggling to pry itself from his body. I could see that with my right eye. My left eye, meanwhile, looked out a door that led to fields of green, a blue sky, trees, and abundant life all around. Birds chirped as they darted from tree to tree, celebrating in the symphony of spring. In that moment, I knew everything was divinely timed and let go of wondering how long it would be before Dad stopped breathing.

The hospice nurse arrived and we sat Dad up on the couch. He swayed and wobbled like he was drunk. He tried to focus and barely whispered, "What's happening?"

"Pappa, you're going to hospice now. The ambulance is coming to get you, OK?"

"OK." He had the look of a sweet, innocent child. "Why are we going there?"

Trying to be strong and show support for the next part of the journey, we stated the truth gently and firmly. "They can take better care of you there, they have nurses and staff. If you need any medications or medical help, they'll be right there. We are going with you, so don't you worry. We'll be with you every step of the way." Then the ambulance showed up to take my father away from his beautiful home overlooking a lake and green pastures that went for miles. He went to hospice on May 16 for two nights. He died on May 18. In the spring, his favorite time of year.

When Dad became ill four years earlier, he had aches but he didn't complain very much. Even after four operations, he never spoke of pain. He would quietly go about his daily activities until he was too tired. The biggest frustration he ever expressed was about the effort it took to walk the dog a block to retrieve the mail.

Dad seemed content with his life, even though he wasn't financially rich or academically accomplished. Most impressively, though, he was unafraid to die. He was at peace with his life. He was surrounded by family and church community. His cup was full.

At this time of Dad's life, the time of completing, there were no worries. He had trust and faith instead of fear. Adam—that's his name—was a great teacher through his simple acts of kindness and service to others. He was hospitable and safe to be with; his interest in being right with God was why he was unafraid to die. He was right with God.

The man I once blamed for my struggles in life when I was younger became the man I turned to for the way to authentically live my life. It is his love that made his children strong.

The greatest gifts my father ever gave me? He showed me how to be unafraid of death and carved a clearly marked path that will one day allow me to follow him home.

⚘ Questions to Consider

There are times in our life when we judge our parents for what we believe they did not give us. Is there something you wanted from your father that you didn't get? Would you be willing to forgive him for not being the perfect dad with the perfect job and the perfect communication abilities? Perhaps he didn't know what you needed, or how to give it to you.

Who would you be and how would your life be different if you forgave him?

If you want to forgive and don't know how, please reach out to a counsellor, minister, or other professional. They will help you become free of the heavy burden of judgement.

Chapter Five

Fern: Being present, a son's greatest gift

A beckoning to the hospital in the middle of the night with a warning that "your mother is taking a turn for the worst" isn't the most assuring introduction into one of the most important experiences of one's life.

The hospital room was cold and there were no windows. It was too quiet, a state that highlighted the bouts of moaning from the dear woman in the bed. The shingles in her eyes made it so she couldn't see, but she could hear.

Her son stood by her side through the night, thanking her for the wonderful job she had done raising her seven children and being a devoted wife. Fern was a kind woman. She was strong in a quiet way and steady in her unwavering love for her family. But now her eighty-five-year-old, lighter-than-air softness was dimming into a flickering shadow. It was time to call the other children and invite them to say goodbye. Flight plans were made instantly and, within hours, her children were surrounding her.

My friend invited me to support him that day, so I drove up and we met at the local diner. We were finishing off our lunch when we got the call Fern had passed. Expecting a room full of people in various states of grieving, we were surprised to find the room empty, with Fern's body lying peacefully among flowers. Suddenly, we noticed Fern's face turning pink. We stood there, eyes bulging out, mouths hanging open. We could feel the essence of her in the room. She had come to say goodbye to her son, who had made this passing so complete.

I left shortly after to go back to the town I lived in, two hours away. Later that day, I was walking on my prayer hill, revisiting the experience. My friend had been up all night with his mother, walking her through and tenderly caring for her. Suddenly, a vision of Fern's spirit descended upon me softly like a butterfly and whispered, "You and my son would make a good team." Then she winked at me and vanished. I felt a chill and a sense of warmth at the same time.

What if my friend had not answered the phone? What if his mother had died alone in the hospital that night? How differently the experience would have been if there was no one there encouraging Fern to wait until her children arrived. They would have all just received a call to say, "I'm sorry. Your mother has passed." There would have been no "Thank you for being a great Mom," farewell words, or family warmth as she ascended into the great mystic.

Since the time of Fern's death, I have moved my life two hours south to be with her son as my husband. I know to listen to the wind!

A man caring for his dying mother is a testament of his character. Fern was elegant and, quite simply, a smart woman. She raised her sons to be gentlemen. She got what she gave and, in the end, her children came to uplift her and share the agony that dying is for those being left behind. Dying is like getting old and, more than once, my late mother-in-law quipped that "getting old isn't for sissies."

We still feel the essence of Fern's gentle spirit. Perhaps she wove her being-ness into our lives with the things she left behind: a stone cross on the wall engraved with "The Lord is my Shepherd;" the plastic roses and dollar-store flowers that we keep in the planters outside to duke out the deer; vases, dishes, and photos that remind us of a woman whose good death happened because her son picked up the phone.

𝄢 Questions to Consider

Is there a time you wish you had picked up the phone and did not? Can you take the time now to make a call in your mind and finish up what you need to say to that person or situation? The person need not be alive for you to do this. Give yourself the gift of rewiring the experience as you imagine the conversation; notice your breath and what other emotions you may be feeling as you freely express yourself. In your mind, allow the other person to receive your words and feelings with total acceptance.

Look that person and the situation courageously in the eyes, and see yourself completing. Sit quietly and notice your breath and if you have emotions that want to be in motion.

Breathe, and let the experience be your teacher.

Chapter Six

Herman: Why is this "dying" taking so long?

The average patient's stay in the care home I was sent to work in was less than forty nights. The man I was hired to care for had been there for more than a year. With a warning that he could be difficult, I perched myself on a chair a few feet away while witnessing a tentative last parting between a father and a daughter. She lived and worked hundreds of miles away, and had braved treacherous winter roads on the weekends. Children in tow or alone, she came to be at her father's side, as loyally as the tide rises and falls.

Bending down to kiss him on the side of the head, she said "I think his medication is too strong. Last time I was here, we walked to the kitchen for tea and went for a sit in the garden. This time, he's just slept the whole time. He's not eating or drinking, he's just lying there, unconscious." Without offering more than I could deliver and barely moving so as not to interrupt their sacred space, I assured her, "I have both eyes on your dad and will give him liquids as soon as he shows signs of waking." Struggling to leave her father's side, she inched toward the door. "Thank you. He loves butterscotch pudding. He'll eat that."

What I knew about my new client was minimal. He was battling more than one kind of cancer and medication was part of his pain management. I heard through the grapevine that, when awake and alert, Herman would challenge the staff, demanding meetings to share his ideas and suggestions to make the place better. Herman was a successful builder, and had contributed much to the community through his church and leadership. He was well-respected, and had a great sense of humor. If you patronized him or were inauthentic, he would call you on it. And even though he was supposed to be dying, he kept a firm grip on who he was as a living being until he died.

Eventually, though, Herman's demands became unsettling for the facility that housed him. Ensuring a calm, peaceful atmosphere for patients and their families was the staff's job; unfortunately, the effort it took to keep it that way with Herman on the loose began to take its toll.

During the first few weeks of caring for Herman, I learned about his wife, who had passed away a year before, and his five children, all of whom had conflicting ideas about what his care should look like. It was a potpourri of opinions, and it felt like a volatile emotional bomb ready to explode at any time—most likely at the most inconvenient of times. If it wasn't Herman himself demanding to speak with the bosses of employees, it was family members arguing bitterly about his too long a stay in this place. There were constant requests by some family members for less medications to be given to their Dad, others wanted him to try different medications or more medications. Some family demanded less staff involvement, others wanted more staff involvement. It seemed as if nothing was changing for Herman; for others, everything was always changing and nothing ever seemed to please everyone.

The situation required self-management. One had to be emotionally balanced with healthy boundaries and skilled in communicating with individuals and families in crisis. The staff pulled out every tool they knew to help Herman die with dignity, and sometimes that looked like frustrated confusion, for no one had ever walked this path before.

It was important to not judge people's fear based and sometimes erratic behavior. Standing back and breathing in awareness about the situation, I could relate to the unworkability and stress from all points of view. Letting the experience be a teacher, I became aware that deflecting and releasing emotional tension was as important as showing up on my game, ready to provide care. When a family member ranted about the behavior or unresolved issues involving another sibling, it was important to listen and focus on positive actions that would create a healing environment.

Herman was moved to a lockdown unit where his behavior and medications were monitored. Herman was so angry that he wasn't dying on cue. "This is not how it's supposed to go. When you are told that you are at the end of your life, you expect the dying to happen in a timely manner," he would say.

The not knowing was very stressful for family members. They cancelled vacation plans because they didn't want to miss their Dad/Grandpa's passing. A revolving door of visits from family and friends became the norm, and I could see that Herman was becoming more agitated.

Twenty-four months passed, and it seemed that the dying process was on hold as the living process became regulated. Herman was now simply existing. Each day looked the same: medications, breakfast, a nap, maybe a visit with one of the kids or a church member, lunch, another nap, another visit, dinner, meds, then bedtime. His physical body was being managed, yet there was an explosive anger that lurked beneath the surface. Herman's frustration would manifest as a dinner tray flying across the room, or slamming bathroom doors with him successfully locking himself behind them. Safe from our suggestions that he eat his carrots or take his meds or get into his PJs, he would shout abusively through the door at those of us entrusted to care for him.

Herman would often speak of his wife, and how much he missed her, after she passed away the family was in shambles. Having their father diagnosed with a terminal illness right after their mother's death had complicated the family's grieving process, and they really didn't know what they needed to do. Live their lives as normal? Put everything on hold and sit at their father's side to wait for his last breaths? What if another family member was visiting— was it safe to go in and risk a fight over unresolved issues? They wondered "Do I stay away and suffer silently or fight for my space to be with him?" Each family member struggled differently, all of them bearing the weight of uncertainty, some hunching over as if to protect their aching hearts, others suffering headaches from the pent-up emotion that furrowed their brows. Some children smelled of vodka when they visited, and sat silently while their dad slept. Other family members chatted non-stop to avoid those painful silent gaps where reality ached its way through anticipatory grief.

The closer death came, the angrier Herman became. It was as if he didn't trust where he was going, yet he had a strong faith and said he knew he would see his wife, mother, and father and that made him happy. Finally, one day, I asked him, "Why are you so angry? Do you even know?" With the saddest downcast eyes, he spoke in a defeated tone. "When my wife died, I missed her so much. All everyone could talk about was how sick I was getting, and how worried they were for me. My kids don't get along and that's not the way it's supposed to be. I didn't raise them to fight and hate each other. They should love one another, even though they are all different from one another. I'm ready to die, but I don't want to leave the kids behind. I don't think they will be OK."

Now we had something to work with. Herman was looking to resolve the conflict in his family before he went to his spirit home. Discussing the issue with the family gave us all a direction to move in. Visits became co-visits, and laughter replaced the hostility among family members. The time in bed for Herman extended to always, with short trips to the toilet when he could stand and walk. Herman was given medication to manage his physical pain; his emotional pain was healing by expressing the need to have his family be OK before he left this planet.

During the last few days of Herman's life, he spoke of seeing angels standing in the room, big purple ones. One afternoon, he said his wife was sitting beside his bed and he drifted off to sleep with a soft smile upon his face. The next day, Herman began to hear the whistle of a distant train. His eyes would be closed, but you could tell he was listening for it because he would stretch his neck out and cock his head to one side. A smile would appear on his face as if he welcomed its arrival. Once Herman took the stand that there were no favorites among his children, that they were all his favorite, the sibling animosity disappeared.

All of Herman's children and grandchildren were standing around his bed when he was dying, crying and comforting one another. They became the family he had raised them to be. Job well done, mission accomplished. "All aboard who's going aboard. Choo Choo." The train chugged in, Herman breathed his last earth breath, and got on.

⚘ Questions to Consider

Do you remember a time in your life when things did not go according to plan? Did you experience fear, doubt, and certainty that things would turn out badly? Or did you trust that everything would be fine? Where in your body do you hold emotion that is wanting to move but can't seem to express itself? Breathe into that place and smile at the recognition of emotion wanting to move.

Chapter Seven

Helma: Life is about the intention of love we put into our living

The room was huge. In the center sat a woman of ninety-two, her humble presence emanating a graceful serenity. She was basking in the beauty of watercolor poppies, magnolias, and breathtaking sceneries painted on canvases all neatly placed around her. Pallets and brushes were strategically poised, patiently awaiting the students' arrival.

"Is it OK if I join your art class?" I asked, pulling up a chair. I had always wanted to learn how to paint.

This spirit-filled woman and I became friends. Both of us suffered from the same faith, and enjoyed sharing stories about the wrath and wonder of life. She had been married to the same man her whole life and had two beautiful kids. I met them and they were great people. Helma would give me useful counsel about marriage and how to be successful at it. I was a couple of years into my third marriage and about to crash and burn it like the other two, repeating patterns of unworkability. But thanks to my wise friend, I began to see things from a different perspective. She literally saved me from myself. We would often pray together and our friendship became a source of spiritual food that we both savored.

Snow flurries threatened the night I popped in for a quick hello to find Helma in bed looking very sad. Wishing that visitors would knock on her door, she longed for those days when people bustled with the busy-ness of life in a place they knew as home. There were no words to offer as she spoke of this silent pain called loneliness. We just sat there with the truth that her heart ached. The monster of loneliness was eating up her time and we needed a recovery plan. The following week Helma invited a few ladies over for a visit and to see some of her art work. My job was to assist with tea and the maneuvering of wheel chairs since each woman needed help with mobility. Four giggling grandmothers sharing life stories seemed like a safe place, so I asked them "What did you love most about the men you married?" Their response was not something I expected. They all said the same thing: "They had gentle spirits, they were gentle- men." It made me appreciate that I had finally gotten it right. My man is a gentle spirit too, not spineless. That's different.

When my third anniversary came around, I didn't know what to get my husband as a gift. Helma suggested I paint him a picture and then she offered to be my coach. The watercolor poppies she helped me paint turned out beautifully. My husband's favourite part of the piece is a little yellow bud that Helma painted, just to get me started. "This is how much water you need, and this is how much paint you need so it doesn't run but gives you good texture." Helma was a serious teacher, and her warm, sparkly blue eyes took the nervous edge off being a beginner.

There's something comforting about being in the presence of a powerful person who you know can take care of things as life throws its curve balls. Helma was one of those capable people. She could soar through a crisis like an eagle, making it look effortless and just part of the glide.

People can help us change for the better just by their being-ness. Looking back, this gifted artist, mother, and widow was an angel who was waiting for *me* that day. Her authentic, sincere, brimming heart full of love embraced me in a mentorship where I was safe to explore the places in me that needed work. I had no idea how dysfunctional I was, including being in denial about some unresolved personal issues. I was running, fighting, overworking, distracted, and clinging to old belief systems that clearly no longer worked. I did everything but stand, face, and challenge my unhealed pain. Trying to outrun my shadow had been a great strategy for a while, but, let's face it, when you hit middle age, things from the past with which we have not made peace can become burdensome.

Instead of judgement about my ruthless dysfunctional independence, my sage friend gave me suggestions about how to be a better wife while staying true to my heart. Instead of complaints about the challenges of becoming aged, Helma gracefully lived each day with the lightheartedness of a happy bird in song. Her calm certainty, if it were a color, would be indigo blue.

I didn't know when I walked into the big empty room that day it was full of potential, stories, prayers, wisdom, friendship, and new beginnings. Helma, over time, taught me to trust myself. She taught me to trust my paintbrush and paints, which would instinctively know what to do if my intention was loving.

When I respectfully asked her if she was afraid to die, she said, "God has me in the palm of his hands and I need not worry or fret because he's right here right now and knows exactly what he's doing." Then she closed her beautiful soft blue eyes, took a deep satisfied breath and exhaled. Helma was practicing surrendering her life force with love and trust and she was showing me what that looked like. Then it dawned on me, she wasn't teaching me to paint watercolors, she was teaching me how to live and die, I was *her* canvas.

✿ Questions to Consider

Is there a time in your life when you knew you were hiding, not facing an important issue? If so, without judgement, consider this. Perhaps you did not have the skills to navigate such an experience. Perhaps the experience happened to teach you what you did not know. Instead of seeing the experience as something to be ashamed of, "What if the experience becomes your teacher?"

Get a piece of paper and draw a line down the middle. On one side of the page, write down how you feel because a certain experience happened. On the other side of the page, write down the things you've learned and how you've grown because this certain experience happened. Keep adding to both sides of the list. After some time, revisit the list and see if the situation, person, or place has less of a charge emotionally. Do you have a different perspective now that some time and reflection has passed? If you need support to work through difficulties, please be courageous, take good care of your most precious self, and seek professional guidance.

Louis Larson

Chapter Eight

Grandma Olga: See you at the bus stop

Clickity, clickity, click, the heels of his shoes on the sidewalk warned of his unexpected visit at two in the morning. Chills prickled up my spine, surges of survival. This was a deceitful, manipulative, and dangerous man. I knew answering the door would be a mistake. I held my breath angrily that the kitchen light gave my presence away.

Then there was silence; he was at my door, listening for a fearful cry with that wicked smile on his face, knowing I was alone and vulnerable. He tapped ever so softly. My heart thumped so hard that immobilizing panic took hold. He had come to harm me.

What happened next is a miracle that comforts me to this day. The little table plant in front of me sighed. Yes, it's true, and you don't have to tell me that plants don't sigh. I know that. But this plant, on this night, expanded a few inches and then let down with a silently unmistakable "aaaahhhh." Instantly, an invisible, soft wind that smelled of coral roses descended downward into my kitchen. I felt a band of safety surround me and the fear began to lose its grip. My grandmother came into my mind and serenity replaced the adrenaline. Grandma Olga had come to protect me. The man left without incident and was never heard from again.

I did not know at fourteen years old how to deal with my grand-mother's brain tumor or that it had come to take her away. Our times together rolling cigarettes, canning crab apples, and playing with marbles on her hardwood floor were supposed to last forever. The reality of her dying was foreign.

Witnessing Grandma lying in a facility, unconscious, covers strewn carelessly over her body, did not reach my heart until many years later. Her funeral in the dead of winter at a small cemetery in the prairies of Canada left me as numb as my frozen toes. I didn't get, when I was young, how imperative my Grandmother was to my development. After she died, I searched relentlessly for unconditional love and genuine kindness to fill the void.

Decades later, sitting at a table with a child of my own, remembering how her spirit had come to protect me, I ached with longing. "Grandma, where are you?"

Not too long ago, I had a dream. I came upon a woman sitting on a bench at a bus stop. There was a lamp post behind the bench. The view was of a still lake with a walkway in front. The environment was still. There was no wind, rain, sun, or other signs of weather. The woman was dressed in a 1940s camel-colored coat with faux fur collar and cuffs. She wore a hat with a yellow brooch and clutched a dark brown purse in her left hand. My curiosity drew me closer to her. There was a smile on her face as she sat patiently waiting. It was my grandmother, and she was waiting for me!

Caring for seniors is my career. What makes it such a valuable occupation is the tenderness I offer these special people because I never got to care for my grandmother when she was dying. I see her in them, though. Those wise eyes full up with experiences, many too painful to share. Instead of complaining, they flash a soft smile, distracting me with an offer of chocolates or mint candies to protect me from the reality that life can hurt. I play along in agreement, but I see their grief, regrets, and sorrows. Some are sick by the many medications they consume to keep death at bay, some are so lonely their walls creak with sadness. My job is to greet them respectfully, touch them softly, and let them know they matter. I am, after all, touching my Grandma Olga.

৵ Questions to Consider

Take a few moments to close your eyes and appreciate your breath. As you become quiet inside, ask, "*Who* that I am aware of is a spirit guide in my life? How have they marked my life? What is the most important thing they have guided me toward or away from? How will I honor that force of protection, support, and guidance now?"

Tips and Tools

For

The Soul's Journey Home

1.   *Keys to living*

2.   *Remember: life is about giving*

3.   *See it, name it, feel it, heal it*

4.   *Tool for self- forgiveness*

5.   *Perspective – look 3 times*

6.   *Ask permission and begin with "I feel"*

7.   *Big Purple Salad Bowl*

8.   *The Birthday Quiz*

9.   *Playful Questions*

10.   *What is?*

11.   *Questions for Consideration*

12.   *Don't know what to do or how to be?*

Keys to living

- Remember to breathe and say "Thank you" for the day.
- Be adaptable.
- Enjoy your sense of humor.
- It's ok to feel your feelings—they are information.
- Don't just seek help, receive it.
- We are here to grow: to grow out of, grow into, grow up, grow old, grow beyond our current beliefs, grow toward the higher way that is encouraging us forward.

Remember: Life is about giving

- Giving in;
- Giving over;
- Giving it space;
- Giving without expectation;
- Giving grace;
- Giving everything;
- Giving unconditionally;
- Giving up what does not matter;
- Giving with a glad heart;
- Giving with trust that it is all in divine order;
- Giving up opinions that are no longer true;
- Giving way for spirit to speak truth into your being;
- Giving invitation for the spirit to work miracles through us;
- Giving self and others encouragement;
- Giving time and space for healing;
- Giving gentle reminders to all mankind that when we are mindful, we make better choices. Breathe deeply on your prayer walk, smile often with appreciation for life itself.

See it, Name it, Feel it, Heal it

See it. Simply observe yourself experiencing whatever emotions are present. Notice *where* you feel emotions in your body, and give them permission to be there. Notice if you want to run, justify, argue, defend, avoid, or deny these emotions. Give that awareness some compassionate space and ask if this is an OK time to see, name, and feel these emotions.

Name it. Name the feelings you are experiencing and, when you label an emotion, ask yourself: "What are three other emotions underneath this one?" This takes reflection time and honesty. You may be challenged as you become awake to emotions you'd rather not experience. Sometimes, it's the label itself that brings who we think we are into question. A memory from long ago where we tagged ourselves "stupid, incapable, unlovable, unworthy" may undermine our confidence when those emotions and experiences were vital steps on the stairway to courage and clarity.

Feel it. Describe how you feel and where in your body you feel the emotion. After a few minutes, step back from your position and notice that, by giving yourself permission to see it, name it, and feel it, there is less resistance, more support for the emotions to move.

Heal it. When we give ourselves permission to see things as they are, name them as we see them, and feel them, there is an opportunity to heal them.

When attempting to heal an old wound, change a long-ingrained behavior, or forgive ourselves or another, it can be helpful to seek professional help. We all have blind spots and, sometimes, seeing things from a different perspective can trigger much-needed change.

Ask Permission and begin with "I feel"

End-of-life situations can be challenging, even in the best of circumstances. One thing that is across-the-board helpful is to ask permission. If you are visiting someone who is sick at hospice or hospital, gently knock on the door and ask, "Is this an OK time to see you?" If the person is at home, *call and find out* when the best time to drop in is, and ask if there's anything they need.

When you want to clear the air, clarify your feelings, or say sorry or thank you, begin by asking permission. "I'd like to share something about how you've helped me in my life. Is now an OK time to do that?" If it's a sensitive or emotionally charged issue, begin the conversation by owning your piece first. You can do this by beginning with "I feel." It creates an environment in which the sharing comes from your heart. Beginning a conversation with "You did this awful thing thirty years ago and I've been wounded ever since" does not create an environment where it is safe to share vulnerabilities. Make room and time for those difficult conversations beginning with the intention to listen with your heart and soul, not just your ears.

Self-Forgiveness Tool

Sometimes, we stay in places with people for too long. Sometimes, we never get the opportunity to have the experiences we dreamed of. Each regret, loss, and disappointment build's up, eating away at our self-confidence and ability to adapt until we don't recognize who we are, where we are going or why. One of the best ways to reboot and get back to our true north is to have an honest conversation with ourselves.

During this frank conversation, we may experience judgements about ourselves or the way we handled things. Appreciate them for the information they provide, and name them. Feel where they take up residence in the body in the form of tension, anxiety, and blockages. Begin to ask empowering questions like, "What's the most important thing I can think, do, or say that will show love for myself, even though my life doesn't look like I want it to?"

End of life is a time to complete with honesty and integrity. It's not the time to carry the blame torch. No matter how right we think we are, or how justified we feel, the offering of forgiveness regarding people, places, and situations that have not met our expectations is a gift.

Reflection, correcting, and moving forward need not take up years of time in a therapist's chair; however, it is essential on life's journey to consult with friendly forces. Align yourself with people who see the good in you, who uplift you, and empower you to become your best.

Take a piece of paper and draw a line down the middle. On the left side, write down what self-judgements you are experiencing. On the right side, write down how you would like to feel about yourself, including an action you can take right now to support your well-being. Keep adding to both lists until you feel complete.

The key here is to be totally honest and compassionate with yourself. Change can be difficult, so can facing oneself. If you need help, seek it and receive it.

Perspective - Look three times

Settling in the jacuzzi for a deserved soak and needed quiet time I cringed at the sight of him. Noticing the swell of anger rise-up, replacing sought serenity, my teeth clenched and my normally friendly disposition curdled like cream left out on the counter overnight.

This guy seemed to show up at the most awkward times, just as I was getting on a conference call or lying down for a nap and now today without any notice, almost intentionally, I thought, trying to ruin my private spa day.

The first time he drove by the jacuzzi on his lawnmower machine I cursed him silently. I wondered why he insisted on showing up when he was least welcome and deemed him a stupid man with no sense of timing.

The second time he drove past the jacuzzi, bits of shredded grass flew about and I wanted to ask him to leave, well, ask is the wrong word. I wanted to demand that he get out of here right now and leave me to my quiet peaceful time which he had already ruined by his mere presence.

The third time he approached with his whirling bits of grass I noticed something that had not registered before. This man whose name I did not know was about 75 years old and looked a bit like my father.

My father passed a few years ago at 77 and we used to tease him about how much attention he bestowed on his lawn. When Dad became ill, mowing his lawn somehow made him feel better. Watering his lawn gave him purpose in the evenings and fertilizing the lawn was proof he could still take care of things.

As the bubbles frothed around me, tears formed in my eyes. Here I was sitting in judgement of an old man doing his job. It was almost 100 degrees outside and he was taking care of business while I sat my lazy buns in the jacuzzi cursing his efforts. The words from the bible "Forgive them Father, for they know not what they do" pounded in my heart and seared my soul. Suddenly, the all about me spa day was not so important. Wrapping myself in humility and a soft towel as I got out of the jacuzzi, I shouted at that man who was now driving away on his lawn rider. I needed to yell, get it out, because that's what I felt so compelled to do from the moment I perceived his presence as an intrusion. "Hey you there! Mister on the lawn mower, wait." He stopped and turned around, bracing himself, preparing in case he needed to face one of life's bitter moments.

"Just wanted to say you did a great job on the lawn and sure do appreciate all you do to make the place look so nice, thank you sir," my voice quivering with the memory of my Father's tenderly cared for grass.

He did not respond with words, just a simple wave of his hand and a smile as he wiped his sweating brow and drove away.

I look for the lawn mower man now, and one of these days I'm going to ask him if he believes in heaven and if he does, when he goes there if he would say Hi to my Dad for me and let him know my grass is green and happy.

Question: What makes you cringe, run, cower, avoid, deny and want to shout at someone for just being present? If you look at them from a new perspective who do they remind you of? How can you acknowledge them for their gift and authentically appreciate them? How much better do you feel about yourself when you shift your perspective from judgement to acceptance?

The Big Purple Salad Bowl

Do you remember a time when you went off the rails, raging on your soapbox about politics, religion, or someone's behavior? After some time passed, I'll bet you looked back and wondered who or what had taken over your body and made you rant like that. Sound familiar? Not you, hey? OK, sure. I'll give you that. If, for some reason, an experience such as this happens to someone you know (not you, of course, because you're emotionally in control all the time), this exercise can be very helpful.

If you are the person witnessing such a human expression, sometimes the best thing to do is let the person rant for a reasonable stint of time.

Imagine this person's tirade being dumped into a big purple salad bowl. Sure, for all the things you dreamed of becoming in your life, a purple salad bowl may not have even hit the radar. However, for the sake of helping another back into balance, you are one now.

They will vent up one side of the issue and down the other using various tones as they play their emotional instrument. From anger to rage to disbelief to justification, they'll spew out their opinions, spurred on by something someone has said or done. After some time, exhaustion is bound to set in. No one, after all, can sustain a powerful emotional vent forever.

You may be most helpful when someone is expressing themselves by simple active listening. Salad bowls don't have to fix, negotiate sides, or offer other ways to see issues. They receive whatever is coming in without judgement. "Oh, good," they might just as well say. "More stuff for the salad."

I have learned after decades of working with people that human expression, no matter how passionate, shifts after it is received authentically. People can get off whatever issue they're on when they can hand it off to someone who's willing to take it. Sometimes, it's better to kindly witness, listen and let it all filter it into your big purple salad bowl self. None of their emotional issues get on you and it feels pretty good to get them out.

Birthday Quiz

Sitting with a person who is dying can be uncomfortable and confusing, as there is no standard manual for doing it right. Every person involved—from the person at the end of life, to the family and friends, and all the people in between—has a unique set of needs they're trying to have met. Everyone is trying to get it right. The staff, if there are any involved, are doing their best to give good care. Supportive family and friends visit with flowers, cards, and expectations of some kind, spoken or not. In the end-of-life stage when the person dying is still alert and conversing, this tool can be useful. Through the Birthday Quiz, we get to explore the peak positive experiences in one's life, the favorite times and adventurous exploration of strengths that helped this person overcome adversity.

Pick a category you would like to explore and begin by asking a question. You may play with this for as long as you like, enjoying the stories, discoveries, and meaningful memories.

What is your favorite?

- Food
- Recipe
- Scent
- Flavor
- Song
- Season
- Color
- Flower
- Tree
- Place you've travelled
- Musical group
- Actor
- Actress
- Movie
- Song
- Book
- Author
- Poet
- Instrument
- Time of day

Playful Questions

If you were a tree, what kind of tree would you be?

If you were a flower, what kind of flower would you be?

If you were a dog, what kind of dog would you be?

If you were a cat, what kind of cat would you be?

If you were a car, what kind of car would you be?

If you were a pair of shoes, what brand would you be?

If you were a body of water, would you be: a dew drop, a still pond, a meandering stream, a sputtering rain shower, a calm ocean, a stormy sea, a thunderstorm, or a raging river?

If you could learn a language in a day, which language would you choose and why?

If you could visit any place in the world, where would you go?

If you held a goodbye party and could invite any person or any pet, living or dead, mythical or real, what would that look like?

<u>What is?</u>

One of your greatest strengths?

One of the most treasured gifts you've ever received?

One of the most important gifts you've ever given?

The mindset that helped you get through a difficult time?

One thing you'd like to do over?

One of the nicest things anyone has done for you?

One of the kindest things you've ever done for another person?

The most important thing you need to do right now to be at peace?

Questions for Consideration

The following questions and suggestions are independent of each other. Consider them food for thought. Go at your own pace.

- Unresolved issues? Ask yourself the following: "Who will I be and how will I be different when this issue is resolved?" Closing your eyes and breathing deeply, let the seeds of this thought settle your inner chatter. Allow yourself time as you *patiently listen for the answers.*

- What are three important things you want the person who is dying to know?

- If you had a do-over in your life, what would that look like?

- Are you ready to practice "forgiveness of the self?" What is your first step? Please refer to the tool for self forgiveness in this section.

- If you close your eyes right now and do a reality check on your stress level, where are you? How do you relax even though things aren't as you would like them to be?

- Who do you need to be right now to support a good outcome?

- If you weren't trying so hard to push your agenda and be right, what would dominate the situation?

- How do you support the process?

- How do you clean up the mess you made?

- How do you empower someone else to clean up the mess they made?

- If you weren't angry right now, what would you be?

- If you weren't afraid right now, what would you be?

- If you weren't in such resistance right now, what would you be?

- What is the most important thing you can do or say to bring harmony right now?

- Is there a time in your life that you were hiding, not facing an important issue? If so, without judgement, consider this: perhaps you did not have the skills to navigate at that time. Perhaps this experience came to teach you what you did not know. Instead of seeing this experience as something to be afraid or ashamed of, let it be your teacher. Take a piece of a paper and draw a line down the middle. On the left side, write how you felt when the experience happened. On the right side, write down how you've changed because of that experience. Keep adding to both lists—there's no time frame. When there's no more to add, ask yourself if it will benefit you to seek professional help to resolve this and move past it.

Don't' know what to do or how to be?

There are times in our life when we don't know what to say or how to be, not because we lack desire, skill or compassion, but simply because we are in unchartered territory.

Participating in the walking home of a family member or loved one could be one of those times when we don't know what is the right thing to say or do.

Keep in mind that silence can speak effectively, and its ok to not use words when we are communicating. A soft touch, a nod of the head or an agreeing sigh can be more meaningful than dialogue.

If there are many people present at one time it can be effective to use a ritual to bring everyone onto the same page. Lighting a candle, covering the patient with a favorite blanket or placing objects in places where they can be admired are small actions that show we care without using words.

If you don't know what to say or do, simply owning it and bringing it to the table is real and acceptable. Its ok not to know, and its ok to say you don't know.

Think about the person you are walking home and ask yourself; What can I offer this person in the way of word or deed that will provide comfort? What ritual is appropriate that will honor their life journey and this sacred time of closure?

Ideas for positive closure may include; listening to favorite music, decorative night lights, flowers, saved letters and cards from cherished ones brought in now to rekindle the memories. Articles of clothing, handmade or purchased on vacations, will serve as physical reminders of those special times. Jewelry, books, photos and favorite objects will carry weight and comfort too when words are hard to find.

Stories, yes, do tell stories at end of life and ask questions too. As the time draws near and the person is preparing to leave their body ask no more of them. Simply *being* with the dying person as they ascend can be a comfort. The greatest gift you can offer a dying person is to *be a safe zone*, supporting them to "rest peacefully in your presence" as their spirit makes its way back home.

Cindy Bertrand Larson and her husband, Terry

About the Author

Cindy Bertrand Larson works as a New Decision Therapist, a cherished role that sees her helping the sick, aged and dying, along with their support networks. She also teaches a workshop for individuals recovering from drug and alcohol addiction and is a facilitator, keynote speaker, puppeteer and author.

Bertrand Larson lives in the Sonora desert with her husband, Terry, and her cat, Sheba. The nature preserve that serves as her backyard, and the beauty of its abundant lakes and trees, give her much joy. Bertrand Larson takes great satisfaction from knowing that she, too, is a piece of the natural world. And she embraces her own journey toward death with sincere gratitude for the breaths she continues to draw.

She has written *End of Life Stories* to reach out to readers in a state of pain, loss, grief and uncertainty. She hopes that her words find troubled individuals as those of a trusted friend might, and that they provide genuine comfort in a difficult time.

About the Illustrator

The illustrations in this book are original works by a man named Louis Larson, a.k.a Luigi. With no previous skill in the creative arts, Lou picked up a paintbrush at ninety years old and created more than twenty original paintings. Some of them are included in this book.

Cover photo by Judy Lloyd whose gentle persuasion and unyielding belief co-created this first book in the series of *"End of Life Stories."*

CPSIA information can be obtained
at www.ICGtesting.com
Printed in the USA
LVHW01s0452100318
569342LV00002B/2/P